W9-ACG-662

HISTORIC PRESERVATION IN INNER CITY AREAS

A Manual Of Practice

by
Arthur P. Ziegler, Jr.

THE ALLEGHENY PRESS PITTSBURGH, PENNSYLVANIA

FIRST EDITION

MANUFACTURED IN THE UNITED STATES OF AMERICA
LIBRARY OF CONGRESS CATALOGUE CARD NUMBER 72-171721

Contents

Foreword

In 1964, in Pittsburgh, I was among several persons who established an activist historic preservation organization called by the unwieldy but descriptive name "Pittsburgh History & Landmarks Foundation". Our goals were to "preserve the significant architecture of Allegheny County and educate people about our local historical heritage."

The organization was fortunate in having a board of directors and an executive committee composed of individuals with strong principles and clear minds, and several staff members who were willing to devote themselves fully to our cause without concern about their immediate remuneration. We set about to make our views known to the public and to governmental agencies, and we immediately began to outline the reason for our disagreement with certain urban renewal policies and to propose positive alternatives.

In Pittsburgh we were blessed (the word is very apt) with private foundations that invested in our proposals. We also were bolstered by some gifts from private individuals. During our early years corporate, union, and broad public contributions were minimal, but that pattern is now changing.

With these funds and backed by our determined board and an enthusiastic and growing membership, we attempted to devise programs of all kinds to preserve the buildings we loved and to enliven local history. The best elucidation of these programs occurs in our *Five Year Report, 1964-1969.*

Among these efforts is a series of neighborhood restoration programs that gained national recognition for one unique feature that differentiated them from many other historic district programs; we endeavored to utilize historic preservation of houses and shops as a means to renewing the civic pride of the people who lived in the area and to involve them in the restoration activity rather than dislocating them. This principle committed us deeply to community action work as well as to architectural restoration, and through continual trial and error and abundant learning, we slowly defined some practical principles to meet varying community situations in areas in which we wanted to restore and preserve the architecture.

One of the great needs in the preservation movement is to make such learning and experience available so that others can build on it rather than start all over again.

To that end the National Advisory Council on Historic Preservation, the National Trust for Historic Preservation, and the Pennsylvania Historical and Museum Commission called a national conference in Pittsburgh in September 1970 to review this work.

The conference had an unusual format: we did not import specialists in historic preservation to lecture. Rather we journeyed out into the neighborhoods and met with neighborhood people who did the lecturing, and we invited extensive audience discussion with them.

When the conference ended, we had many requests for a transcript. Those requests together with the constant flow of requests for information that flow into our office compelled us to comply.

When we transcribed our tapes, we found that the discussion had been so informal that the text could not really be very useful to people who were not present at the conference. It was difficult to determine who was speaking, often there were interruptions, and all in all, while the conference was very useful to those who attended, it had little use as a printed record.

I therefore decided that perhaps the best course of action was simply to write a little, practical manual of our principles, directions, and experience that other persons and organizations might like to review for their own work. Much of the manual derives from the splendid discussions of our participants at the conference. Some of it results from my study of the excellent work of other preservation groups, and a considerable portion comes from my own work with the Pittsburgh History & Landmarks Foundation.

For the concept of "recycling" old buildings I am indebted to Professor Robert Stipe, who used that term to describe the Pittsburgh work. I am, as always, beholden in all of my work to my friends, mentors, and allies: Barbara D. Hoffstot, Charles Covert Arensberg, and James D. Van Trump. All photos, unless otherwise noted, are by Charles W. Shane.

As is generally the case in my work, I am heavily indebted to others for the substance of the matter, but the formulations of attitudes and opinions are entirely my own.

Arthur P. Ziegler, Jr.

Be it ever so humble . . .

. . . there is no place like the home neighborhood. (Photo: Courtesy Alcoa)

I. Start With Principles

One of the misfortunes of the historic preservation movement in the United States is that most preservation groups are born in contention. They start with an issue, and usually belatedly. A governmental agency or private corporation or individual is about to demolish a structure dear to the hearts of some local citizens, and they get angry. Generally they have no trouble mustering forces from a large segment of the community. Probably they are right and equally late; they should have spoken up many months ago when the original plans were being laid, but the reality of the loss only became clear to them at the last moment. A hot battle ensues, tempers fray, feelings are hurt. Often enough the preservationists win a stay of execution until they determine whether they can find resources sufficient to assume ownership of the structure or another solution. Sometimes they do, sometimes they don't.

But all too often in the public mind, once the issue has died down, the luster of the preservation group tarnishes. Somehow the members frequently become identified as starry-eyed idealists without a notion of practicality, or as contrary-minded, progress-stopping intransigents, or at best well meaning but uninformed and vaguely dizzy Romantics. Forever they are identified as the group that tried to save the old Renaissance federal building (a heavy-handed, blackened impediment to more parking, whitened at the edges by pigeons) or as the benign, harmless restorers of Grandma Nonesuch's log house built sometime during the past 250 years.

Preservationists always have enough obstacles to overcome without conveying an image of general perversity and light-mindedness. Seldom is any government agency, any highway department, any corporation desiring land for expansion, any city council, any labor organization, or any neighborhood group automatically on their side.

Yet historic preservation has made positive contributions to many major American cities far disproportionate to their

Decayed Victorian urban row housing with pleasant architectural details offers restoration possibilities.

Do we do this?

Or this?

limited size and niggling resources. And there is hardly any city in the country that can do without their message, their practicality, their information, and their Herculean energy. *In order to make their contribution, preservationists must learn to start with principles rather than issues.* They must start forcefully, and they must let the community know that they mean business, but first and foremost they must delineate their goals and their potential contributions to the community and then communicate them clearly to the public.

I do not mean that like an Urban Redevelopment Agency a preservation group must map out a great master plan that encompasses the city and will take innumerable years to implement. That would be a hopeless beginning.

I mean rather that the group should show the community what architecturally valuable districts and structures it has; not only should such structures, such districts be clearly noted, but their aesthetic qualities and their *usefulness* must be fully described. The group must enthusiastically point out how these landmarks can continue to serve the community through specific new uses or revived uses.

After all, any city can build new areas; funds from Washington are available, planners can be appointed, progress when defined as newness, as "the latest thing," can easily be advanced. Few communities will fail to subscribe to any plan giving them, as it were, the latest model.

But while good modern buildings can be designed and built today, no community can create an historic architectural legacy; by definition that had to be created by earlier generations, and those earlier styles are no longer part of our active architectural vocabulary. Architects are no longer designing Greek or Gothic Revival houses, Italian Renaissance city halls, or French Second Empire fire halls, Victorian churches, or Chicago-school office buildings. (Unfortunately they do design an endless proliferation of American Georgian buildings!) Even more important, the unique artistic and humane qualities of historic neighborhoods cannot be recreated. And by attrition and destruction, such areas will continue to reduce in number.

Insensitive to the landscape and the neighborhood, such high rises for low-income people are often imposed upon a community that is completely unadjusted to the living patterns they represent. (Photo: Judge)

This renewal scheme represents a magnificent willingness to invest in the renewal of Pittsburgh's decaying North Side by a major corporation but unfortunately it called for almost total annihilation of the existing architecture. The removal of all former shops, houses, and people, and the development of a fortress-like structure repels residents of the surrounding neighborhoods and deprives the new residents of the area of a direct perspective to the nearby river. In spite of some excellent contemporary design "within the walls", this kind of renewal violates the traditional living patterns of people, tears up their roots. (Photo: Courtesy Alcoa)

You must involve the community in your plans.

Yet it is to just such neighborhoods that, in principle, most Americans feel loyal; they will tour them when on vacation, read about them, tell their children about their importance, show them to visitors, feel that "somebody" ought to be saving some of them, and in some cases they will even live in them. (An interesting statistic would be to total up the number of hosts who show their guests local urban renewal districts and the number that show them historic neighborhoods.) At the same time these same people complain, and rightly so, of the dehumanized quality of many modern developments, both commercial and residential.

Often, however, local citizens fail to recognize that their own cities contain their own equivalent of Williamsburg or Philadelphia's Society Hill or Charleston's Ansonborough. They need to be shown that architecturally valuable neighborhoods exist in their town, too. That is why I emphasize that *the first duty of an historic preservation group is to ar-*

ticulate to a community its indigenous architectural values. People want to believe in and love their hometown; their response will be favorable when they hear its unique values being extolled.

Preservationists are in a particularly good position to undertake such educating. Frequently they are intelligent people, who can effectively present their views. Second, they love their area and have a keen sense of its historic importance. Third, they firmly believe in the utility of historic buildings. And fourth, they know and are concerned with the total city. They are not fusty antedeluvians busily preoccupied with genealogy or misty events of the past; they are committed citizens who want a healthy, interesting, useful, and pleasing environment. They are worried about dirty air, befouled waterways, benighted bureaucracies and the general ugliness and dehumanization of modern life. They will consign many hours of effort to improve the community with no thought of personal aggrandizement.

That is why preservationists must start their organizations before they need to fight. Their goal must be to obtain positive accomplishments that serve the entire community, and that is best obtained by beginning with a program, not a battle; the latter will happen often enough. As a preservationist, you must begin thoughtfully, asking where the buildings and the neighborhoods in your city are that have architectural character and potential viability that can enhance life, and then demonstrate in general terms to your fellow citizens the principles in which you believe and for which you will fight.

Your principles should be firmly rooted in the relevance of your historic areas to your local architectural scene. Perhaps your town lacks a Society Hill or an Ansonborough; that doesn't matter. The question is only what is valuable in the context of your town; perhaps, like Toledo, Ohio, your oldest areas are largely Colonial Revival (built c. 1900-1915). Then these are what you should deal with. You must investigate your city's buildings and determine which ones really are of significance in the context of the city's development, and then tell your fellow citizens about them.

II. Why a Preservation District?

The principles of your program must be grounded in facts. They must derive from a rationale that is clear and obviously sound and that makes sense to your fellow citizens. Here are some basic reasons on which you can base your argument.

1. Massive demolition is unworkable

The first reason for preserving historic districts is a practical one. Our cities simply cannot handle the logistics of dislocating the vast number of people that would be required were we to demolish all of our old and decaying neighborhoods and substitute new ones. In my own county, Allegheny, the second most populated county in Pennsylvania, 90,000 out of a total of 503,000 dwelling units need rehabilitating. Of these no one quite knows how many might be considered architecturally worthwhile and therefore susceptible to restoration rather than simple rehabilitation. (Rehabilitation can be defined as renovating the structure to make it fit for habitation once again; restoration goes beyond that to include retaining and refreshing its original exterior architectural character and as much of the original interior as possible; it adds a dimension of special value beyond that of structural soundness.) This figure includes only residential structures, not commercial, governmental, religious, or others. Across the nation more than 5,000,000 houses are in desperate need of rejuvenation.

If we were to mobilize all of our available forces in this field to replace these units, we still could not begin to cope with the problems. Pittsburgh, for example, has been a leading city in the attempt to renew urban areas through the clearance approach. Yet in the first 25 years of urban redevelopment, less than 2,000 acres have been renewed out of 14,000 needing renewal now and out of total land area of 35,330, and not a single project has yet been completed. At this pace we will need 120 more years to renew the remaining areas that require redevelopment today. To annihilate all of our decrepit dwelling units in Allegheny County (20% of our total supply) simply to build up new ones would be a mammoth endeavor. And where would the displaced residents live in the interim?

Preservation, on the other hand, recycles the structures that are there. It does not require taking down the existing bricks, windows, basements, and floors, hauling them away, and bringing in new bricks, windows, lumber, and block and building them up again. It is therefore faster and creates less dust, debris, and noise to try the patience of neighbors. Often work can be undertaken while residents in a house stay on. Perhaps a renovated formerly vacant home can be occupied by a family while their original deteriorated dwelling is restored. Utilities do not have to be relocated, streets remain intact and, most important, patterns of life essentially continue as before.

In fact, neighborhood morale is *vitalized* by restoration activity within the area, while massive demolition destroys that morale as well as the buildings. Very few human beings really enjoy seeing their home area wiped out, but all like to see it renewed.

2. *Preservation bolsters morale*

That point suggests the second good reason for preservation: it renews the human spirit. It has always seemed obvious to me that if a public agency enters a neighborhood saying, "Your houses are so deteriorated that we must move you out and demolish them," the emotional result has to be negative. Put yourself in the place of those owners and ask yourself how you would react. But if instead that agency came in declaring that "Your neighborhood has great architectural and cultural value to our city and we must find a way to upgrade it," the result will be positive. Yet almost never has the latter been done by public agencies, although recently they have begun to move closer to it. But it has cost considerable money, years of abortive effort, and violent civil disorders to change their attitudes.

The truth is that architectural decay and human decay go hand in hand. One helps to cause as well as feed upon the other. Reduce one and you deter the other. Never work on one without attending to the other, because without the improvement of both, neither can survive.

Before and after restoration by Pittsburgh History & Landmarks Foundation in the Mexican War Streets area. This restoration of a major building, once so decrepit, was a positive major step, visible from the street. for old-time residents in the area and it also attracted new, young tenants.

A drawing prepared by a staff architect of Pittsburgh History & Landmarks Foundation showing specifically the work required for restoring the facade of a house in a low-income area. This is one of a series of samples made in connection with a program being developed by the Urban Redevelopment Authority of Pittsburgh. It called for facade easements to be acquired by the Authority on a massive basis in this area so that exterior restoration could be taken on a large scale. The traditional loans and grants associated with rehabilitation programs of the Department of Housing and Urban Development are to be made available to owners so that they can improve the interiors and mechanical systems of their homes.

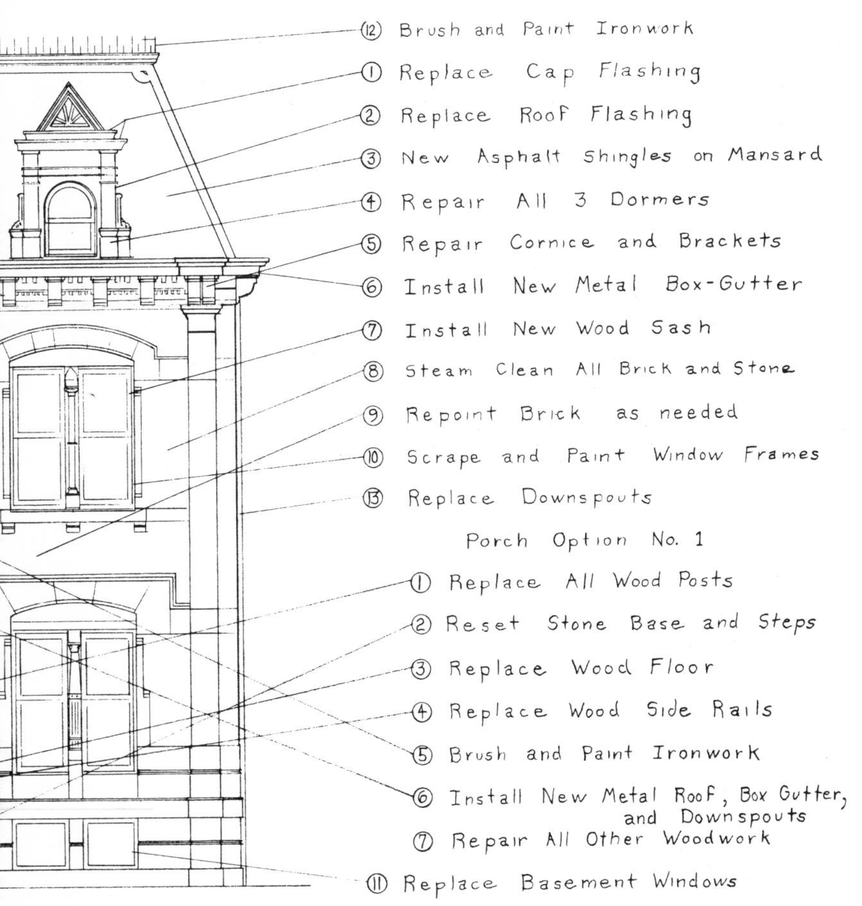

1315 Liverpool Street – Class A

Of course, rehabilitation also renews neighborhoods with minimal dislocation but it does not provide the same morale boost that preservation does because generally it is offered as an economical method of housing improvement rather than a means to save a valuable cultural resource.

3. *Preservation offers aesthetic satisfaction*

The third reason is that buildings that have architectural value please the eye and engage the mind. As our cities grow more dehumanized, as our suburban dwellings become more redundant, as our supply of old buildings dwindles, we find the older architectural styles becoming more and more important. Finding a cluster of Gothic Revival houses is a major and pleasing discovery. Looking at stained glass windows or Italianate cornice brackets is quite diverting. Walking the streets of an historic district becomes a significant experience for thousands of people. The past way of life beckons to us with its harmony of scale, its variety of style, its closely built urban streets, its rich antiquity. People do not necessarily long to live in the past; they need rather a mixture of past and present, a reminder of the way things were and an escape from the less attractive aspects of our present cityscapes, or they simply want to enjoy the foil and counterfoil of past and present juxtaposed. These things a city should indeed provide.

4. *Preservation provides financial benefits*

A fourth reason for preserving old neighborhoods is financial benefit. Restoration helps cities financially in two ways. The first is from increased taxes. We have a strange real estate tax system in this country. It is based on a simple principle: the better the condition in which you maintain your property, the more society penalizes you with increased taxes. Or the reverse: the worse the condition in which you maintain your property, the more society will reward you with reduced taxes. Behind this grim arrangement you can see the leer of the slumlord, forever paid off by society for engaging in his repugnant business.

The tax inequity not only breeds slumlords; it often precludes useful private investment in rehabilitation and restoration. In the past few years a number of small private non-

A pleasantly designed mantel over a fireplace that has ceased to warm the room or the heart.

profit rehabilitation corporations have sprung up in many cities. With scanty resources they are willing to tackle the major problem of renewing old housing. But when their goal is to rent to low and moderate income families, the cost versus income is always very close. The fact that their taxes may be raised, even doubled, when they complete their work on a house or group of houses, combined with the fact that the assessor will not estimate the increase in advance of the rehab work, deters these groups. On the first house restoration that Pittsburgh History & Landmarks Foundation was involved in, taxes were doubled when the work was completed. We had spent $60,000 restoring this particular slum property, but this unfortunate tax increase severely affected our financial return, which was already small.

So you will frequently be asked: what will happen to my taxes if I restore my home? You must truthfully answer that the chances are that they will go up. But so will property value. That is your only rejoinder. If the taxes are higher, obviously the house is worth more. You can also point out that the person who restores his house might, through that act, inspire his neighbor to repair his house, and then both will enjoy an improved environment. His commitment might become contagious.

Historic restoration brings a second financial benefit to cities: tourism. A foundation official once advised our organization to begin putting plaques on buildings because, "Everywhere you put a plaque twelve Americans will appear in the first half hour to read it!" He was referring, of course, to the insatiable interest in history that Americans have developed.

Here are some useful statistics, quoted from a study undertaken by the National Trust for Historic Preservation and Pittsburgh History & Landmarks Foundation and written by John L. Frisbee, III. (Copies are available from the National Trust.)

> In every state, tourism is one of the three largest revenue producers.
>
> Historic sites are an important element of this growing trade. A survey of members of the American Automobile Association showed that 81% named sightseeing as a major recreational activity in vacationing. AAA recommends that a vacationing couple budget $36.00 a day for food, lodging, tips and gasoline.
>
> An estimate for metropolitan Philadelphia is that at least one-fourth of its $250 million a year tourist and convention business is attributable to historic sites.
>
> The Thomas Edison Birthplace in Milan, Ohio (population 1,400) brings over 25,000 visitors to town. The general area has fifty motels.

In a recent survey, the Ohio Development Department concluded that a community attracting 36,500 visitors a year could expect to receive an additional $777,000 in personal income through 111 new jobs, $144,300 in bank deposits, and $1,119,908 in added retail sales.

The James K. Polk birthplace, operated by the State of North Carolina, had 24,500 visitors spending more than $100,000 in the community in 1968. With the multiplier effect of the dollar filtering through the local economy, that $100,000 generated $163,000 in retail sales and provided approximately $14,000 in state and local taxes. Taxes accruing to the state exceeded operating expenses by more than $3,300. The total economic benefit to the community—21 additional jobs, $109,000 in increased personal income and $168,000 in added sales—offsets the costs of developing and promoting the site.

These statistics can be multiplied yet higher for historic districts because they tend to draw an even wider visitation than many single sites. They offer more local services to at-

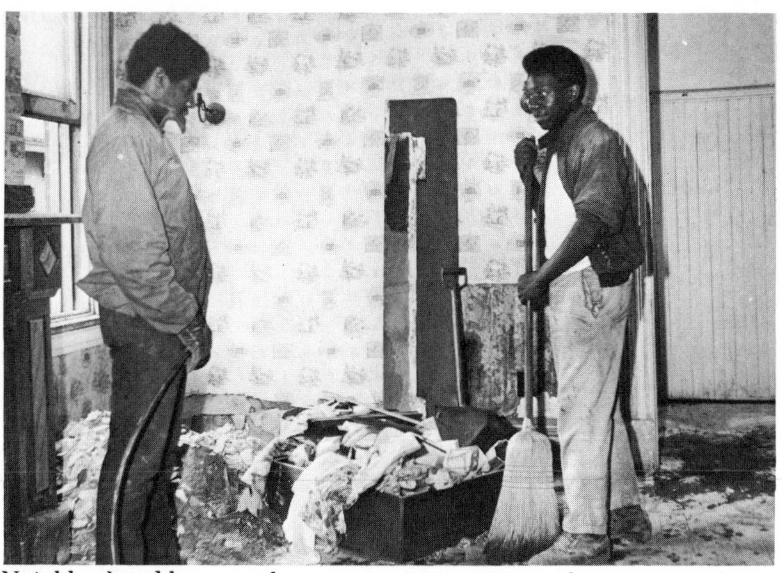

Neighborhood boys can be given useful work to do to contribute to a program that restores their district.

Bad plaster must be removed and replaced with fresh plaster or wallboard.

Often new closets have to be built in these structures and can be located in a variety of places.

Only a blow-torch and scraper will remove layers of paint from old doors.

A highlight in some of the apartments in one house in the Mexican War Streets area is the fireplace walls where the plaster has been stripped off, the brick brushed and pointed and left exposed.

tract the tourist dollar, such as restaurants, shops, and pubs. Also their size and complexity invites more protracted visitations.

Attracting tourists depends on more than having an historic district, of course: good back-up facilities like shops, restaurants, and motels, other major attractions, and an interesting street life must be available. But the statistics above are relevant to any proposal you would make in your locality for historic district development.

5. *Preservation unifies community forces*

Another reason on which you can build your local case for historic preservation is that it often utilizes more community resources than does demolition. I do not so much refer to the suppliers and contractors who will furnish the materials and carry out the work; I mean the human resources. If wiping out neighborhoods to build new ones really does result in disheartened or angry citizens, certainly those citizens are going to expend considerable energy battling the authorities instead of helping them. The authorities in turn will lose time and money in this bickering. Historic preservation, however, brings out the positive aspects of human nature. Individual citizens will pitch in and help; community organizations will lend their support and their muscle to help the local public agencies wheedle money out of state legislatures and Washington; private corporations and labor unions will provide technical assistance and funds; private foundations will donate to the cause. Historic preservation is one of the few urban renewal efforts that I know where the private sector will spontaneously help public agencies. Even teenagers have been known to go to work rehabilitating houses as an alternative to dropping out of school. (See Frank Trippett, "On the House", *Look Magazine*, December 29, 1970, pp. 67-69.)

Build on these fundamental principles as you develop your case for preservation in your community. Relate them to your specific circumstances and add to them as appropriate, always remembering that the arguments for historic preservation are not simply theoretical. They have been tested and found to be true.

Some views of "restored" apartments renting to moderate-income persons and families.

Rents for such units range from $110.00 to $200.00 with the largest number of them for between $125.00 and $150.00 per month plus electric.

The frightening "before"

and the rewarding "after".

III. The Basic Steps

We next turn to ways and means of implementing historic district restoration in an inner city area. We will assume that you have established a private, non-profit organization for this and perhaps related purposes, and that you qualify for private contributions under both Section 503(c) of the Internal Revenue Code and Section 4653 of the Tax Reform Act of 1969. If you have not yet developed such an organization, you can obtain excellent guides to help you do so from the National Trust for Historic Preservation.

We will also assume that you have delineated the neighborhoods for which you wish to develop restoration programs. If you have not yet conducted an architectural survey for your area, contact your state preservation liaison officer for information, and perhaps, for matching funds to do so. Write your governor's office for his name. The Historic Preservation Act of 1966 authorizes federal grants to the states on a matching basis for such surveys. We will assume that you have completed your survey.

The question before you then is how to begin your district restoration program. The steps are simple enough:

1. Publish your general architectural survey as a book. That form of publication will give you authority in the community and your survey work will seem more substantial and permanent. A book will also enjoy wide distribution, and you must reach as many people as possible.
2. Make a commitment to one or more of your proposed restoration areas (which you delineated and described in your book) by meeting with the residents, then by announcing your program to the public and raising funds for it and, as soon as possible, by acquiring property in it to be followed with actual restoration by your group or by reselling your acquisitions to persons who will restore them.
3. Keep the news media informed of progress so that the public remains aware of your work and has a strong image of your district.
4. Work with planning and other city agencies to protect

the area and improve city services. Try to obtain passage of historic zoning for your area. For information on such zoning see Jacob H. Morrison's *Historic Preservation Law,* published by the National Trust for Historic Preservation.

5. Try to maintain a good relationship with the people already living in the area so that they become allies rather than opponents who feel that you are "taking over" their neighborhood.
6. Have tours and special events in the area for your members and the general public to help promote it.
7. Assist those who want to improve their property or to buy and restore property with obtaining mortgages, FHA Home Improvement Loans, special FHA loans for low income families, and architectural advice.
8. At every opportunity be enthusiastic about progress being made, but recognize frustrations and failures so people believe you have a realistic recognition of the complexities involved.
9. Do not try to administer the district authoritatively. After all, once the district is well on its way to completion you and your organization should move on to other projects. *The area should belong to those who inhabit it.* You must guide the program from a distance, offering advice when it might be taken, letting people find their own way when it won't. If your hand is too heavy, your residents, new and old, will resist your influence. Many of them will have acquired property under your program in part for the sense of adventure, of the pleasure of pioneering, and an authoritative attitude will deprive them of one of their primary motives for participating.

In our next few chapters we go into some of the details of implementing such a program.

IV. Revolving Funds

In order to carry out a major historic district restoration program, you will probably want to establish a revolving fund to finance your work. Broadly defined for preservation groups, a revolving fund is cash or other equities, a line of credit or any combination of these owned and administered by a non-profit organization for the express purpose of purchasing and restoring architecturally significant structures. It can also be cash loaned by a nonprofit organization to individuals or organizations for the same purpose. All proceeds from rentals, sales, interests and dividends must be returned to the fund in order to replenish it. Thus the fund revolves. Generally, such funds are used in specific urban areas and districts rather than applied helter-skelter to one building here, another elsewhere.

Revolving funds can be of great use to you. First of all, revolving funds tend to focus an organization's attention and resources. Money collected in a fund is generally designated for a specific area and cannot be used later elsewhere. On the other hand, an organization has the freedom to determine expenditures within the area, thereby having the latitude to use its own discretion in working on specific projects.

Second, revolving funds attract donors. Donors like to see their money working, and when a project is finished the donor can see exactly what his contribution helped support. Like gifts to endowments, donations to a revolving fund are in a sense perpetual because they are returned through sales and rentals but unlike endowment gifts they are more obviously in continual and full use. They are not simply earning dividends and interest; the principle itself can be expended without being used up.

Third, the revolving fund can act as a substitute endowment, to which administrative costs can be charged. Ten percent of a $250,000 revolving fund allocated for administration costs can be quite significant in the operation of your organization.

Finally, preservationists need power. Without it legislation cannot be effected, bulldozers cannot be stopped. The quickest way for an organization to gain political influence is to show its power on the street by buying and restoring, selling and renting property.

Of course, the first question is, where do you get the money? You might as well learn now that you do not drop a line to the Ford Foundation outlining your needs and anticipate a handsome grant to your cause. *Your funding must be local.* If you seek major revenue in establishing a revolving fund, you really have only two choices: make a request to one or two or three major sources or mount a broad community campaign. Or, you can always start small: $6,000 and a mortgage will give you a nice start.

The broader your community financial support, the better for your endeavor. I have found in Pittsburgh that while approaches to major foundations for major revolving fund grants have been looked upon with favor, their response grows if we can return later and show that we secured small donations from business, labor, the average citizen. You will find it a general rule that in attracting large sums, two things are extremely useful: the first is a specific, concrete proposal outlining your goals, the rationale for the program, methods of implementation, and carefully projected budget. Second, collections of dimes and dollars already in hand from smaller organizations and individuals impresses your prospective grantors with the favorable community commitment to your work. In the latter instance it is not the total amount that is important; it is the number of donors.

In order to raise funds, you must assess your own situation. Ask these questions. How should we begin our program? Should we buy one house and restore it or should we secure a number of properties? What amount of money will it take to demonstrate that we can handle the job? Exactly what are the funding sources in our community? How large are their gifts apt to be? How many different sources can we canvas? Can we raise funds not just from corporations but from labor unions? How about the local independent businessmen; to what extent do they have a stake in what we are trying to do? How much can we raise through individual and family memberships?

The answers to the questions, and others equally obvious, will provide you with the answer to the initial questions of where you get the funding. It is really not an esoteric matter. When you set your board of directors, include businessmen and civic leaders on it so that you will have the benefit of their advice. If your proposal is solid and will really benefit the hometown, then you must convince the hometown to support you.

Five Types of Funds

There are at least five pertinent and different types of revolving funds. They are not the only options available and can be changed or combined to meet specific needs.

1. *The Charleston Fund*

   Charleston had the first revolving fund for preservation in the United States, and it has been wisely guided by Mrs. Frances Edmunds. The principles of the fund administered by Historic Charleston Foundation are, in general, to buy a property, restore its facade and offer the building for sale. By restoring the facade the fund controls restoration visible from the street and improves the appearance of the neighborhood even if no one lives in the property for a time while a buyer is being sought. The view of the facade from the street interests private buyers, who most often are eager to apply their imagination to the interior of the building. In recent years the Charleston Fund has tended to buy large rows and clusters of buildings to gain added protection. With the resales goes a restrictive covenant in the deed prohibiting changes to the facade. This procedure of the Charleston Fund has been used with enormous success.

2. *The Savannah Fund*

   Savannah also has one of the first—and certainly one of the most successful—revolving funds, one that is ingenious, easy, fast and in its way inexpensive. Like Charleston, the Historic Savannah Foundation charts out a district, usually in the downtown or inner-city area, and acquires property there. Historic Savannah then promotes the area, publicizes it (you may have seen their national ads in *Antiques Magazine*) and involves particularly the Junior League and the business community in building up the public image of the area as a place to live. People, perhaps those thinking of moving south, as well as localities, are induced to buy an historic house in Savannah and restore it themselves.

Historic Savannah established guidelines and restrictions for restoration in the historic areas. A covenant in the deed prohibits changing the facade for 99 years and is transferred with any future sale of the house. A local preservation ordinance backs up the Fund by requiring a special permit to alter the facade.

The point is that the Savannah Fund is concerned simply with buying, promoting and selling. That fact is borne out by the selection of their director: not a preservationist, not a historian, Mr. Reid Williamson was an eminently successful promoter for local industrial development before assuming his office with Historic Savannah. Together with Lee Adler, a successful businessman who steered the organization as president, he and his organization have shown that sound business principles can produce a handsomely restored inner city area.

The Pittsburgh Fund

My organization, the Pittsburgh History & Landmarks Foundation, (PHLF), has a different kind of fund. Begun in 1966 with $100,000 and now totalling about $500,000, the fund has been used in a variety of ways. Our group is one of the few organizations that works on the interiors as well as the exteriors of buildings. In most cases the buildings are restored both inside and out (although changes are made on the interior) and then rented. They are rented for income purposes, of course, but also because it enables us to provide dwelling units at a variety of rental rates. The buildings are mostly in inner-city, decaying areas. The exceptional aspect of the PHLF effort is that we make a commitment to try to retain the people who live in the areas where we acquire property and we try to develop residences for all income levels within the same neighborhood.

A case in point: We moved into an area that we deteriorating badly but that had not yet reached full ghetto conditions. We first acquired a house in poor condition and invested considerable money in it, and then rented it to middle-to-moderate income groups, particularly young people who could sustain themselves and bring fresh vitality to the neighborhood. In the process we had to dislocate tenants from this overcrowded dwelling, but we found new homes for all of them, several nearby. We also asked our members to buy some of the properties and to restore and rent or move into them. More importantly, we urged as many property owners as possible to stay in the area and repair their buildings. In fact after four years of work in this area, we and our members have still not purchased any homes except those owned by absentee landlords. We also restored houses and rented them to the Pittsburgh Housing Authority, which in turn sublet them to poor families at subsidized rates. This effort is described in detail in Chapter VII.

In another area, our revolving fund was used to buy some badly blighted houses in an otherwise reasonably sound inner-city district to prevent the decay from spreading. We are restoring these for low income families.

Explicit in PHLF's use of the revolving fund is an effort to make old buildings function in a modern city—a changing city—and for all income groups. While some of its restored properties are rented to moderate-to-middle-income groups, others rent under the leased housing program to low-income tenants; we get our investment returned in about 15 years. Not a quick profit, but we are fulfilling our goal of saving valuable buildings, improving the environment, creating fit habitations, and serving low-income families. So far, there have been no racial problems in our integrated neighborhoods.

Using a revolving fund in this manner entails large expenditures and the training of a restoration crew or the development of a sensitive contracting firm. We have been fortunate in developing our own work crew but at times we also utilize outside contractors.

4. *The Revolving Loan Fund*
Although they are not preservation funds, two others deserve attention. Both were developed in Pittsburgh. One is administered by the Neighborhood Housing Services, Inc., a non-profit group established by the American Institute of Architects, the Homebuilders Association of Western Pennsylvania, the local Chamber of Commerce, the North Side Civic Development Council, PHLF, and local banks. Neighborhood Housing Services, Inc., does not buy, sell, or restore. It lends.

The organization was set up in a neighborhood containing many valuable Victorian buildings, most of them owned by the residents rather than by absentee landlords, and most in need of repair. Property owners, prodded by a code enforcement program in the area, acting on their own initiative contact NHS for help in getting loans for their improvement projects. An expert from the organization inspects the buildings and makes up a specification sheet of exactly what is needed. Cooperating local banks have set up a high-risk loan fund for such projects, but if for some reason the owners don't qualify (too old, too poor, too many financial obligations), NHS extends the loan. In its first three years of operations only one borrower defaulted, and only a minor sum was involved.

5. *The Major Development Fund*
The other Pittsburgh revolving fund is the Action Housing Development Fund. Action Housing, a non-profit civic group set up about 15 years ago, was established to improve the supply of moderate-to-low-income housing in Pittsburgh. Action Housing has no interest in historic districts or in architecture *per se*, but it does have an interest in creating good housing.

Unlike preservation groups that tend to think small and stay small, Action Housing set right out to establish a

$1,600,000 development revolving fund to enable it to lend money to contractors to cover their start-up costs or to finance other aspects involved in developing new or rehabilitated (but not restored) housing. The contractor pays the usual interest rate for the loan, but he gets money from Action Housing that for various reasons he could not get from a bank; the money is returned to the Fund at the time he secures his conventional or FHA mortgages for actual construction.

Where does the organization get its money? Partly from foundation grants, but also from borrowing. Action Housing relies heavily on corporations in Pittsburgh to allocate money on call. Suppose that the Fund needs $50,000. Let us say that XYZ Corporation has allocated to the Fund $200,000, which it keeps in-house until called for. Action Housing borrows a pro-rated share of the $50,000 from XYZ at 4% a year and lends it, say, at 8%. The difference pays the total operational costs of the Fund.

Action Housing is a nonprofit organization, just as preservation groups are. Yet it thinks big. Why couldn't a preservation group interest a contractor in restoring a 12-block area in a city or town and lend him the start-up money he needs from such a revolving fund? The contractor would get money he couldn't get from a bank (which would perhaps be timid about the location or condition of the housing) and the group would obtain the restoration of a whole area rather than, as is usually the case, only a house or two possibly doomed to be ruined by the decay of the rest of the neighborhood anyway.

Let me now offer briefly some advice on how to use a revolving fund and attract the money and keep it coming:

1. Survey and define geographic areas on which you want to spend the money and set up clear-cut goals; but leave yourself open for change.
2. Promote. Use the news media to inform the public about the architectural value of the neighborhood. Produce television programs, publish brochures, get some articles

in the newspapers, involve the Junior League. Take your lead from Savannah.

3. Be flexible in your work and your attitude. Government programs change all the time and cities change practically overnight. You must be ready to respond. Don't fix your means of implementation in so permanent a way that you cannot easily respond.
4. Charge overhead and promotion to the fund.
5. Keep your money invested when it's not in use. Don't let it rest in the bank; keep only what you think will be needed for any 30-day period. Buy a certificate of deposit, buy commercial paper. Don't buy stock, which can fluctuate quickly. Keep your money available.
6. Publish financial reports and reviews of your accomplishments regularly and submit them to your main donors.
7. Use your money. Buy property as fast as you can with it, if that's your aim, or lend it out. As soon as you don't need all the money you have you won't get any more. If you didn't use all the money you solicited for the purpose you had in mind, you didn't need it. You'll find that people pick that up very quickly!
8. Think big.

V. *Creating Community Support*

The goal of your organization in the historic district is simply to save and restore the buildings. It is not a task you can hope to accomplish alone. A revolving fund will never be large enough to enable you to do so. You must arouse and cultivate the interest of sensitive private persons together with that of the residents already in the area so that they will do it. Your revolving fund is but a tool to help you accomplish this goal. It gives you the opportunity to set examples and standards of restoration, it enables you to acquire property, and to have ready cash for emergency conditions like saving buildings from a speculator or from demolition. Also a revolving fund makes possible your acquiring structures that are in such poor physical condition that they will not attract private investors.

Most important, a revolving fund gives you a physical presence on the streets and injects courage into those who might like to restore a building but would not be willing to undertake such work on their own.

Neither the old-time residents who have been watching the particular district decline for several decades nor outside investors and potential residents who know the area to be deteriorated will venture into investing in property restoration alone. How will their investment be protected? Why should they move into such an area as a single pioneer, with no resources to attract others?

Your revolving fund solves that problem. By careful acquisition of houses in strategic areas, you provide anchor structures which in turn create security for individual investment. For example, if a long-term resident lives next to a slum property, his thoughts are necessarily on leaving, not investing in his house. However, if you buy that slum house and restore it and bring in good tenants or buyers, the family next door that has lived for so many years in the neighborhood will then be more inclined to remain and repair their own house.

By carrying out a particularly fine, perhaps even grand restoration you will not only induce new and more affluent residents to come to live in that house, but you will also bestow a certain tone (at times almost a sanctity) on surrounding property. "I live next to that magnificent house that the Landmarks group restored," would not be an uncommon remark.

In short you must use your funds to provide anchors in the neighborhood. As soon as one spot or one street is progressing on its own, that is to say that private persons are restoring without fear of losing their investment, you should stop purchasing there and move along to the next street, always developing a solid field of private commitment behind you. Remember that you are not there to purchase houses in order to make money for your organization; you are there to spend it on behalf of the architecture.

Before you even begin, however, you must convince the community, including the neighborhood in question, that your program will benefit the community and deserves support. To begin, find out who the neighborhood leaders are and meet with them to present your goals. Involve them in the planning, particularly that of communicating the plans to the area residents. You might find it desirable to establish a citizens' advisory board. Include representatives from residential, institutional, and business organizations in your area.

When you present the proposal to the entire neighborhood, the most effective sales tool is to show slides of the area, slides of buildings they see each day, that they inhabit, and describe their architectural value. The response is generally one of shock over what they haven't noticed, haven't valued, together with gratitude toward you for opening their eyes.

Then be specific about how you will implement your plans, with their help; cite financial programs available as outlined in Chapters IV and VI. Assure them that one of your first priorities is to tackle slumlord and derelict properties. Describe the willingness of public agencies to help the program.

Follow this meeting up by releasing news to the press and television highlighting the architectural values of the area and explaining your restoration program designed to save them. This kind of public attention will help to verify in the neighborhood's mind your enthusiasm for their buildings. It will also elicit interest in the area from the larger community.

A landmarks organization is forever popular with the press. You will find yourself in almost an heroic position because you are not only trying to spruce up your local architectural heritage, which gives the citizenry pride in the hometown, but you are reversing decay in inner city areas and providing better housing both for current residents and possibly for a certain number of newcomers who can be very useful to the area and to the city at large. You may be attracting back into the city an intelligent group of individuals who will want to improve the quality of urban life. They will try to help both the city and their neighbors.

You should develop continuing relationships with individuals at your newspapers and television studios. When you have a story, let them know. When an unusually fine or unique restoration has been completed, invite them over to see it. Try to interest the papers in feature articles on individuals and their motives in coming to the area or to old-timers who knew it in its grander days, observed its decline, and now, incredulously, are watching its comeback.

In Pittsburgh, one television station arranged for a newscaster to take a walk through a restoration area with an official of the landmarks organization and the two simply talked about the area, design characteristics of the structures, and the restoration program. A year later people still remembered the program and were asking that it be shown again.

Another useful device to obtain publicity aimed at attracting broad community interest in your area is to hold luncheons or cocktail parties in houses to celebrate a completed restoration, and invite the news media and public officials in. Also, do not overlook the editors of small community papers outside your historic area. They will often be grateful for such an unusual story, and through them you will obtain coverage in other neighborhoods for your own area. At the same time don't ignore the current residents; a backyard party for everyone might be useful.

As restoration proceeds, you should encourage those who restore houses to invite members of organizations to which they belong to see the completed work and perhaps to have some punch or a meal. The garden club, the Kiwanis, the bridge club, the ladies' church guild, all of them would enjoy such an extraordinary experience.

At all times be alert to possibilities for special events. In Charleston, South Carolina, for example, a full week is set aside each year for house tours, including a candlelight tour. It is publicized mightily, and draws thousands of visitors. In Historical Fallsington, Pennsylvania, a Christmas season tour has become a useful event. Other areas hold flea markets, art shows, spring house tours. All such events bring public notice to your area, bestow prestige on it, and create in the public mind a sense of the vitality of the neighborhood; people will begin to say to themselves (and more important, to one another) the action is *there*.

You should also publish a brochure on your historic district program. It should outline the architectural value of the area, summarizing its history, state your goals and methods of implementation, and describe your need for support from the neighborhood as well as the larger community. It should be modest enough to enable you to pass it out at no cost and in large quantities.

Furthermore you should publish an annual report that candidly discusses progress and plans and sets forth expenditures for the past year and the proposed budget for next. This report should be distributed to the news media, civic and public officials, and your members. Keep the information flowing, keep the community informed.

VI. Developing Your Historic District: Low to Moderate Income Residents

We are assuming that your historic area is in an inner city area and therefore largely occupied by low to moderate income people, with much of the property being owned by absentee landlords, often slumlords. Because the more affluent social classes have forsaken the district (except perhaps for older persons who do not wish to leave their long-time homes), the poor have immigrated to it, and the slumlords, by ruthlessly sub-dividing the houses and permitting endless deterioration (that way they're rewarded with those property tax decreases) have been enjoying a good return on their meagre investment. In a sense, the neighborhood "belongs" to those who live in it, however, and you owe to these residents a chance for them to remain there, while recognizing that some occupants will be compelled to leave if overcrowding is to be reduced. At the same time, you will probably need to bring in some more affluent and more highly educated residents in order to help the neighborhood achieve fresh vigor and improved ability at self-determination.

There are only two ways to carry out historic restoration without dislocating all low-to-moderate income residents: minimal restoration work and subsidies for costs, rents, or sales. Very probably even minimal restorative work cannot be utilized for the desperately poor because even minimal work in badly deteriorated dwellings still creates rentals beyond their reach.

Minimal restoration work has to be defined by the condition of the given property. First, the property must be basically sound and have at least some reusable mechanicals. For example, if exterior walls are bulging so badly as to necessitate rebuilding them, or if the electrical, plumbing, and heating systems cannot continue in service, minimal restoration will not work.

Your investment can be reduced by retaining and freshening up old kitchen equipment, leveling and sealing old floors with a synthetic trowelled-on material and by salvaging bathroom fixtures by erecting drywall in front of the old walls and reaffixing the fixtures. In the latter photograph the plumbing can be saved if a new wall were simply to be built around it.

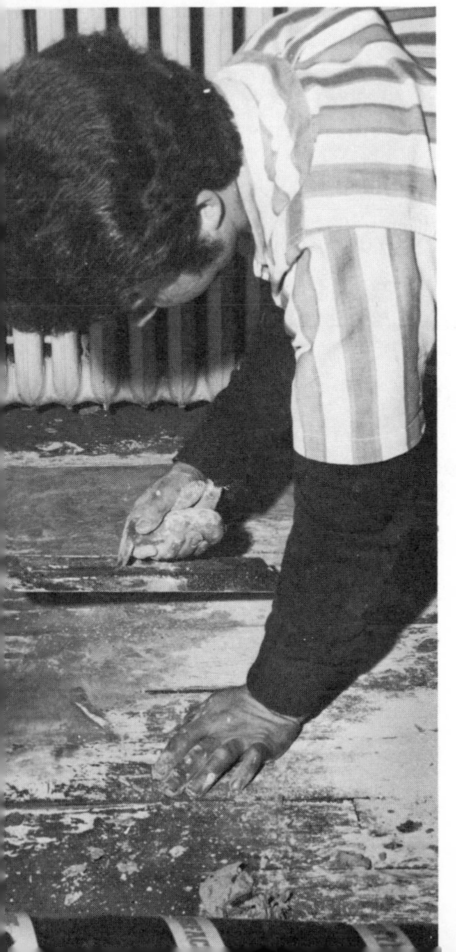

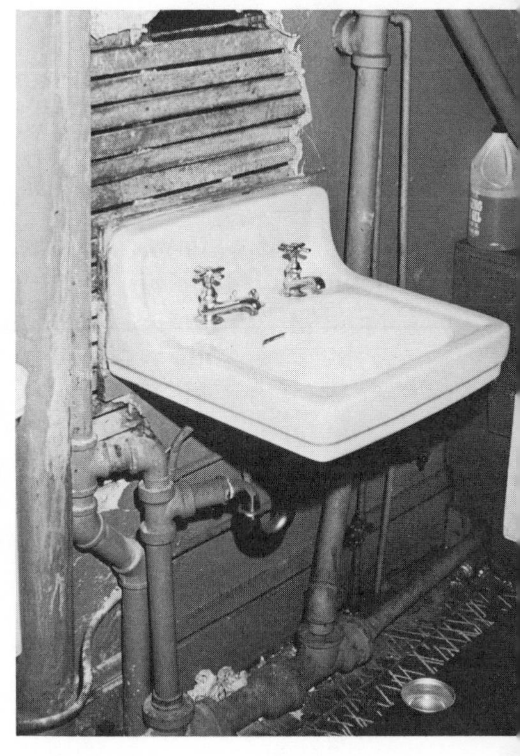

Termites had digested much of the beams in the basement of this ghetto house.

Here are a few examples of corner-cutting to achieve minimal restorations.

Stud old interior walls and sheet with drywall rather than replastering.

Paint over old wallpaper if possible.

Scrape and paint old floors.

If a floor covering is required, use linoleum.

Use rubber stair treads, not carpet, on hall stairs.

If new bathroom plumbing is needed, do not tear up the old floor; lay the pipes over it and build a raised new floor on top.

Keep the existing sinks, bathtub, lights and other fixtures insofar as possible.

Paint woodwork; don't try to refinish it.

Have tenants help with the work, like painting.

Enlist federally funded Neighborhood Youth Corps youngsters to help.

This list is meant only to indicate the direction in which you should be thinking. Other economies will manifest themselves as you work. Obviously minimal restoration work should be done only where full funding cannot be obtained and only as a temporary (1-5 years) measure. It is not a final solution but it will enable you to save more buildings and improve the living conditions of the residents without unduly disturbing the rental levels, and you spread your money further.

For a more useful and permanent solution, you must utilize a federal subsidy program (or that of a state or local government if available). These are few in number and niggling in appropriations, but they do exist and you should make every effort to tap them. Described below are some of the more pertinent ones.

1. *Rent Supplement Programs*
   "Under Section 236, National Housing Act of 1934 (as amended) federal assistance is provided in the form of periodic payments to mortgagees to reduce mortgagors' interest cost for reduction of rents or cooperative charges for those tenants unable to sustain the economic rent." In other words, the government can help pay the rent for low income tenants. Contact your FHA office for exact information.
2. *Home Ownership Assistance*
   Under Section 235(i) of the National Housing Act of 1934 (as amended) a non-profit sponsoring organization can finance the restoration of single family and two-family dwellings by obtaining a loan for 30 years at the current FHA maximum rate which can be scaled down as low as one percent depending on the purchaser's income. In other words, the construction loan is subsidized through FHA.
   Under Section 235(j) an owner can finance the purchase of restored housing through an FHA subsidy of the regular mortgage rate up to one percent. The owner pays 20% of his income on the mortgage and as his income rises, the owner's contribution to the interest rises. This is not an FHA insurance or construction program but

This is a view of a living room of an apartment that rents under the leased housing program to a low-income family; it has had the same restoration care that the more costly rental units have

rather a direct subsidy payment.

3. *Leased Housing Program*

   A non-profit sponsor can acquire sub-standard dwellings and restore them to the specifications of his local Public Housing Authority at a rate that returns investment in approximately 10-12 years. The Housing Authority provides a guaranteed lease for five years, assumes all management and routine maintenance, and subsidizes the rental of the units by charging their tenants at a lower rate than they are paying the sponsor.

4. *Housing Authority Purchase Program*

   Under this arrangement you can purchase and restore houses and then sell them to your local Public Housing Authority at a break-even cost. Simply contact your local housing authority for information.

5. *Urban Renewal Program*

   It is beyond the scope of this book to describe the many kinds of programs available if the neighborhood you want to restore is declared an urban renewal area. We

The delights of a do-it-yourself restoration attracted a suburban family back to the inner city. (Photo: Courtesy *News Record*)

are primarily concerned here with restoration work implemented by private organizations and individuals. However, one URA program should be mentioned, that of facade easements. It is possible for a redevelopment authority to purchase easements on the facades of architecturally significant buildings in an area certified for renewal and restore these facades. Then the agency can transfer ownership back to the owners of the structures while at the same time making the traditional rehabilitation grants and loans available to them so that they have funds to bring the remainder of the buildings up to code standards. Although this program has not been widely used yet, the potential of it is remarkable because it means that a large number of buildings could undergo exterior restoration and interior renovation without massive dislocation. Such a program could be carried out in conjunction with a private restoration organization which could provide architectural studies, restoration guidance, and public support.

6. *Tax Reform Act of 1969*

Under the Tax Reform Act of 1969 incentive has been provided for private individuals and limited partnerships to invest in restoring houses for low income people. Such investors may, on completion of such restorations, take a full depreciation of all costs over a *five* year period.

This program could be utilized by your organization if you were to develop a separate, private organization and attract investors. For example, if you could attract ten persons to invest $5,000 in a specific program area through a limited partnership, you could then obtain a mortgage against the proposed restoration work and increase this $50,000 by five to eight fold thereby giving you a total of $250,000 to $400,000 for investment in restoration. Each of the ten partners could deduct his share (10%) of the total investment over a five year period. This means that he could deduct $25,000 to $40,000 over the five years, a sum each year equal to or larger than his original cash investment.

At the end of five years, sale of the property will result in treating all gain as ordinary income. Such a result can be avoided either by retaining ownership of the property or selling it and re-investing the gain in the same program again.

By writing the Department of Housing and Urban Development, Washington, D. C., or by contacting your local FHA and Public Housing Authority offices, you can obtain amplification and specifics of these programs and learn of new ones as they are developed. If your organization enjoys public status, that is if it is an integral part of your local government rather than a private organization, more funding possibilities are available. Also these programs are subject to change and elimination and new ones will undoubtedly develop. Keep abreast of such developments by subscribing to the *HUD Newsletter* ($2.50 per year) and request FHA brochures describing the assistance programs for low-to-moderate income families.

Remember, too, that funds are available for local public agencies through the Department of Housing and Urban Development for acquisition and restoration of buildings of particular significance and through the Department of the Interior for the same kind of work by private non-profit groups. Both programs encourage adaptive uses for the buildings to be restored that will serve the community, such as health care facilities, art galleries, community centers.

A large room has been divided into a dining room and kitchen with a service opening directly between the two.

VII. How to Develop Your Historic District: Bringing in New Residents

We have said that more affluent families will probably be needed to help stabilize your neighborhood and preclude a resurgence of decay. This may not necessarily be the case if sufficient subsidy funds are available to restore your district and to pay for supporting physical and social services. Seldom are they so abundant, however, and I therefore want to describe some procedures that you can follow to attract middle-income families into a decaying area in an effort to create a viable neighborhood with neither total dislocation nor total dependence on subsidies.

My own experience is that in the early stages of development rentors are easier to attract to such an area than buyers. The reason is simple enough: tenants have less to lose than owners so they are more willing to take the risk of moving into a decaying, yet interesting area. Therefore you should begin by developing rental units. Buy a house or two, develop them into apartments (perhaps including two or three in each house), and advertise for tenants. If properly handled, your efforts will bring results. Many young people, for example, do not want to prolong the suburban pattern; they want to come back to the city. They also want apartments with some distinction, some adornment, often some antiquity. They cannot afford to purchase a house and restore it and probably do not want the fetters that property ownership brings. But they have a sense of adventure, and they want to involve themselves in the problems of the city and be exposed to people from other backgrounds and social strata. They will be willing to invest in a year's lease to experiment, and they will therefore have little to lose.

Their presence can bring immediate new vitality to the neighborhood; their rent will enable you to succeed in your risky restoration; and you will be on your way to creating a viable urban neighborhood with a demographic mix. The old architecture will be an attractive and binding element that brings people from different backgrounds and income groups together in the quest to create a special neighborhood where everyone is welcome. Their only common denominator will be their devotion to their historic buildings.

Once you have secured your first tenants, you must keep the work going. Purchase another house or two. (Always purchase all the property you can afford in order to provide as many anchor buildings as possible, even if you can't restore them all.) Announce more restoration work, and begin to "sell" the area to your membership as a place to enjoy the pleasure of restoring a building and contributing in a very personal way to your program and to helping solve contemporary urban problems.

Undoubtedly one or two members will come forth, funds in hand, to restore a house for rental purposes as well. They will be motivated primarily by the promise of the project, by the contribution they will be making to your program, and they will be bolstered psychologically by the hope that they will, in time, get their investment back. In the meantime, their tax bracket will probably be such that the depreciation will be useful to them. These well-to-do, intelligent, and civic-minded entrepreneurs constitute your next rank of zesty pioneers. You cannot proceed without them. And you will discover them only by promoting your area in the ways that I have mentioned in chapter five. Have tours, television programs, lunches in the district, newspaper coverage, and report often to your membership on your progress through your newsletter. (If you don't have one, start one now.)

Next you must begin to capture the interest of people who will buy and restore houses for their own residence. These are the most difficult persons to find because of the extent of the commitment required. They are committing themselves not just to a tentative period of residence or to a sizeable monetary investment; they are relinquishing their home and consigning life and fortune to the area. Once the die is cast, they cannot readily return to their former state.

These people are elicited from many different sources.

Two of the early groups will be new people and couples moving to the city and affiliated with business or university or cultural enterprises, and desiring a convenient, in-town interesting place in which to live. Because they are newcomers, the stigma of decay that has been attached to your neighborhood will not impress (depress?) them very much. They will see the area as it is now and as it might become, not as what is has been. Your problem is how to contact these people, and again your promotional program will help. While it is improbable that your press coverage will be constant enough to reach such persons, they will be discussing possible locations with others who may be familiar with your work; you should inform all corporations and institutions transferring employees into the city about your program, and word, in short, will get around. At any opportunity you have to show such persons your neighborhood, do so. And provide them with a list of houses for sale and the contact for each one. Make it easy for them to buy.

The next group of early potential buyers is, again, young persons who, as friends, roommates, and young married couples, want to buy a house as their residence (sometimes renting out part of it for income). In each case you will be dealing with persons who have just begun the adventure of adult life; they have few responsibilities and little of the kind of experience that might deter them from such an unusual commitment. They also generally do not have children and therefore the typical urban obstacles of old schools, insufficient playgrounds, and racial animosities will not be relevant issues.

Hopefully, some older, perhaps middle-aged couples will want to come to the area. Sometimes these are people who are weary of suburban inconveniences; sometimes their children are now grown and they are looking for a new interest, a new set of values and aspirations to work toward, and sometimes they are preparing for retirement and want to come back to the city. These people will also make splendid ingredients for your neighborhood. They have the wisdom of experience and a seasoned vitality that will enable them to help you span the gap between your new young residents and your old-time residents. They will also provide a measure of stability because they will be there to stay.

The most difficult people to attract are young families. They will be intimidated by the overwhelming difficulties and hazards of the city for their children, they will fear the inadequacies of the schools, and they will easily follow their conditioned response of believing that the suburbs are the place to live because they are clean and green.

To this group you must point out the compensations of urban life. Note how a child can, say, walk to the museum or library, how he can play in the nearby park, how he will meet a broad spectrum of the community and become more tolerant and more sophisticated about human life; even admit that the child might learn more quickly to fend for himself; certainly he will learn to adapt to a variety of human situations. Point out that the family will have more time to spend together because they spend much less time in their automobiles trying to get to work or the store or events. In short be as positive as you can about the district. Believe in it.

Once you obtain representatives of all of these categories, others will follow. Count your area as established, but not assured. You still need to maintain your own commitment, because the prestige and activity of your organization is creating the image for the area. Plan to keep the pattern of development going for some years, and watch it closely; don't let it swing too far in any one direction. Once it becomes "established" it may become fashionable and that could spell trouble for your lower income residents. Your only means of control will be the way in which you rent or sell your properties and the amount of effort you exert in helping your various income groups to utilize the available means of financing their restoration work. Don't fail the residents who were there before you arrived.

When battling redevelopment authorities, preservationists are fond of quoting Deuteronomy: "Cursed be he that removeth his neighbor's Landmark". Then they themselves forget that the landmark about which they are concerned *is* their neighbor's. Tenant or owner, as a resident the neighbor must be respected.

VIII. The Problem of Neighborhood Self-Determination: A Practical Example

This book deals primarily with inner city historic district work. It assumes that loyalty is due to those persons already living in the area when the preservation work gets underway. It further assumes that the best program is one that develops out of the "givens" of the neighborhood rather than being imposed on it. This viewpoint means that in order for you to create an historic district, you should analyze with great care all the strengths and weaknesses of the area rather than just survey the buildings. It also means that every district will vary somewhat and that the guides that I have established in the foregoing chapters are no more than that: *guides, not rules.*

For example in Pittsburgh, we are working in several different neighborhoods; the architecture is generally of the same vintage but the demographic character of the areas varies widely. Therefore each of our restoration programs differs from the others.

This approach of adjusting to the neighborhood in question, and indeed any approach to restoration by a preservation group that is not indigenous to the neighborhood it seeks to restore, raises the moral questions:

To what extent is the group imposing its own aspirations upon the neighborhood?

To what extent should the neighborhood be free to determine its own fate?

To deal with this very complex problem in specific terms, I would like to review one of the neighborhood restoration programs that we are carrying out in Pittsburgh.

First of all, let us recognize that today community self-determination has become a dominant, even a militant theme. It derives largely from the huge (and hugely unsuccessful in neighborhood terms) redevelopment projects imposed on so many neighborhoods by redevelopment authorities throughout the country between the late 1940s and the late 1960s. The utter disruption, the unhappiness,

This pleasant restoration was carried out by people who had lived in the neighborhood for many years and loved their property.

and the abortiveness of those savage massacres of our cityscape are indictment enough of that soulless process.

Now it has become public policy that neighborhoods are to be involved in the planning processes; it is a legislative fact. Citizens are either to do the planning or advise the planners; their approval is mandatory for renewal projects. But there are problems.

To begin with, it is very hard to say where a community (let us say neighborhood because I primarily want to deal with historic districts) begins and ends. Even if you are able to pinpoint the boundaries, are the people across the street from your perimeter not going to be affected by whatever happens in your neighborhood? Are they therefore not also to be considered? After all, your basic principle for a community's right to determine its own course is founded on the belief that those who are affected by the development should have a governing voice in formulating that development.

Second, what about the transient quality of urban neighborhoods of all kinds? What amount of stability and permanence of residents must a neighborhood have before it has the right to plan for itself?

Third, does an urban neighborhood have the right to this kind of autonomy, as if it were not "part of the main?" For example, you might live five miles away on the other side of town, and yet you periodically visit my area and enjoy it. Are you not a resident and taxpayer of the greater city? As a participant if not a resident in my neighborhood, what are your rights?

Fourth, what about the typical, endemic shortsightedness of many neighborhood people? It is not a lack of intelligence that I am referring to but a lack of information and experience that give one a broader perspective. Frequently neighborhood people woefully lack such a perspective against which to place their local circumstances. They also are generally unaware of previous experience that others have had with implementating ideas and processes that they are considering at a particular time; such information might indicate that the particular idea or

A six page portfolio of the delightful details of a restoration area.

122

process is not workable and that they should try another approach. How do you enable these people to be "citizens of the world" rather than "hometown folks"?

Fifth, how do you keep neighborhood fully committed to implementing the processes they agree upon? Generally the neighborhood groups tend to rally around an issue that threatens the area, and as soon as it is laid to rest, the organization dozes off.

And sixth, how do you obtain a true representation of the neighborhood? A neighborhood organization does not necessarily represent the neighborhood. All too often those who have lived in the area longest attend in the fewest numbers. Frequently those who are loudest rather than soundest carry the day. And not infrequently a neighborhood group splits apart very early over either an issue or personalities and only one faction continues the organization. How do you really obtain democracy?

These are ticklish questions, easy to ask and difficult to answer, and I don't pretend to have the answers: however, I would like to indicate how we are coping with them in one of our neighborhood programs, and at the same time specifically show how one such program operates.

Before doing so, I must unhappily point out that preservationists have been as indifferent (perhaps even more indifferent) to community self-determination as have redevelopment authorities. Historic preservation groups across the country from the 1930s up until today remorselessly removed neighborhood residents regardless of their longevity in the proposed historic district or their commitment to that area. They simply replaced them with well-to-do residents who could understand the value of the structures and who could afford to restore and maintain them.

This pattern was not borne of crassness but of necessity. The oldest and therefore most historic sections of most cities had long ago been turned over to the poor and the slumlords. The buildings had deteriorated; the local architectural heritage was jeopardized. No federal and state money was available, and the only means at hand for preservation groups was to motivate more affluent and educated persons to acquire and restore the buildings and move into them. In itself it was a courageous and rather noble and very successful effort. But it had its unfortunate side, and it behooves us to admit it. Seldom was a thought given to those persons who were being dislocated. Good housing for them was not part of the program. And calling neighborhood meetings to explain the programs and obtain the current residents' cooperation was a courtesy consistently disregarded.

This pattern we have tried to break in Pittsburgh. After being organized in 1964, one of our first areas of concentration was a decaying section of our North Side that we identified as the "Mexican War Streets Area" because General Alexander Hays had named the streets after battles and generals in that war.

It was decaying, but not decayed. That is to say, it needed more time to become a ghetto. But long-time residents were reluctantly leaving and only the poor, the black, were replacing them. It was on the mortgage black list of the banks. For investment it attracted only the slumlord.

We raised a pilot revolving fund with a grant of $100,000 from the Sarah Mellon Scaife Foundation in Pittsburgh and developed our approach as follows:

1. Buy houses in the poorest condition.
2. Restore some of them for a variety of income groups.
   - A. Middle income to try to attract persons with some financial wherewithal, education, and vitality into the area.
   - B. Moderate income to provide decent housing for people in the area and to prove to the Redevelopment Authority that renewal of this kind will work.
   - C. Low income to include the poor in good housing in the area.
3. Encourage our members to restore houses in the area as their home or as an investment.
4. Develop a fresh belief in the neighborhood on the part of old-timers there and get them to restore the facade of their houses. (The interiors were usually already in good condition.)

5. Bind this mixture of people—young, old; well-to-do, poor; black, white—together in the cause of preserving and restoring this unique architecture and conducting this urban experiment of neighborhood renewal.

We implemented this program first by purchasing a house in squalid deterioration, assembling our own restoration crew and restoring this house. Restoration for us means actual restoration of those areas on public view. Inside we alter the houses to produce apartments of a variety of sizes and rentals; we maintain old mantels, woodwork, hardware, and any other historic fixtures. Often, if they are too sadly decayed or missing, we bring them in from houses scheduled for demolition in other areas. After fourteen months of work and an expenditure of $53,000 we rented our apartments—and have continued to rent them—to young professional and semi-professional newcomers to the neighborhood. They bring to the area a deep commitment to reinvigorate it and to participate in this urban experiment. The former residents in the building, (12 people, 6 cats, 3 dogs) we relocated generally to public housing or other nearby housing, all except the owner of the menagerie of animals, who, fortunately, vanished one evening; what apartment he has now populated we do not know.

The goal of renting to moderate income groups was first achieved when we purchased a house near the first one and tackled it. Here we made the economics work by renewing less. While we put in new wiring, we kept the old plumbing for the most part. We retained the old drainboard sinks, and spared ourselves a hefty plaster bill by building a false drywall in front of some deteriorated old walls. We used linoleum rather than vinyl floor covering or carpet. The rents as well as the tenants remained the same.

Low income families are also enjoying newly restored houses. Through the leased housing program of the federal government we are able to buy derelict houses, fully restore them, and rent them to our local housing authority at a rate that returns our investment in 12 to 15 years. The Authority in turn sublets to a poor family at a reduced rental. Their initial five year lease, signed before we start work, enables

This little house formerly had lengthy modern windows installed in the first floor. A more sensitive person, induced to come to the Mexican War Streets area to restore a building, took it back to its original form.

us to obtain mortgage funds. This program is a fine one. A preservation group saves a good piece of architecture, physical improvement comes to a neighborhood, a poor family moves into a good house in an area on its way to recovery rather than on its way down, and the government adds to the available housing supply for low income families without red tape.

We obtained the support of our members primarily by "talking it up." First one venturesome lady acquired and restored a house with reasonable financial success and her commitment helped considerably. She too talked it up! Then another, another, each one encouraging others both on the basis of the pleasure and satisfaction it gave him and to protect the investment he had made. Currently (four years after the program began) seventeen members have purchased and restored or are restoring twenty houses. Rentals have remained, for the most part, moderate, and frequently tenants weather the restoration work and stay on.

The old-timers in the area have stopped leaving and have started repairing and painting. They have found new heart for staying; few really wanted to leave to begin with but they were intimidated by the decay, the fall of property value, and lack of street safety. For the first year they listened dubiously to our glowing verbal pictures and they scrutinized our work. Then they became acquainted with our members—a very educated group—who were investing

This house, restored in the Mexican War Streets area, subsequently was drawn by an artist, and his drawing was printed on special notepaper promoting the area.

A garden block program where a garden club helps local residents plant window boxes adds to neighborhood incentive and civic pride.

in *their* neighborhood, of all things; then they began to follow suit, and in four years, 34 of them have painted or otherwise restored facades.

To date we have spent $225,000 in the Mexican War Streets. Every dollar that we have spent has so far been matched by $3 of private money of members or old-time residents and the ratio is getting steadily higher. This to us is urban renewal—through *RE*-newal not removal.

But goal 5, developing in all these people a new sense of neighborhood with the unifying denominator being restoration of the houses, remains to be explained. From one perspective, this accomplishment is perhaps the most significant one.

After we began the program we held several sporadic, informal neighborhood gatherings to which we invited all residents and property owners. We discussed aspirations and afflictions and resolved on initiating some modest community ventures like a clean-up drive. After these were successfully carried out, we suggested that the area establish a Mexican War Streets Neighborhood Association to include all residents and property owners there willing to pay $1 a year membership, the Society to be operated completely independently of our own organization. In this way we felt that the burden of responsibility for solving local problems would be placed squarely on the shoulders of the local people; they would have to work on their own behalf and not look to us as omnipresent problem-solver and benefactor. We would receive the benefit of having the counsel of the Association, which would be free to advise us on the basis of how the neighborhood sees the issues.

The group was slow in making its way, but now it has a firm foothold. At a typical meeting we have between 20 and 50 attendees and they range from widows and spinsters who have lived in the area for 30, 40, 50 years, to retired couples (also old-timers), to young tenants, to newcomers, middle-aged suburbanites, young professional whites and blacks, wealthy investors, and representatives of both white and black poor.

As a meeting group, the members have caucused with

local school officials, the local police captain, a representative of speculative real estate interests in a nearby area, among others. They have taken stands on public issues (historic zoning, herringbone brick paving, street trees), and they have initiated useful projects including several communal, thorough cleanings of the alleys. Dissatisfied with the quality of education in the local public schools, some of the members are now organizing a private school which all children in the area can attend at whatever tuition their parents feel they can afford.

Most of these people actually have little in common; however, the renewal of this historic district and the goals of this urban experiment have given them common cause and from that has come a humanizing education for us all. Our most notable success is that we suffer from none of the malignant racial and economic hostilities that might be expected from such a mixture of people.

Community self-determination? Not exactly. We are bent on saving these buildings, and to that end Pittsburgh History & Landmarks Foundation as an organization pushes and prods, raises and spends funds, imposes on the neighborhood to the extent to which we own property and therefore control it and also to the extent to which we can present convincing ideas and plans to the residents and owners. But we try hard to be open-minded and responsive to what advice the Mexican War Street Neighborhood Association or individuals in the area offer to us.

Before our arrival, however, this neighborhood had *lost* its ability to determine its future. It was on the ineluctable course of "going bad", like any aging organism. It had lost the means of regeneration.

We provide a new injection of energy, of life, and to the extent that the injection creates certain pre-determinations in the organism, we have predetermined.

Essentially, however, we have really freed—or at least started the process of freeing—this area to determine what it wants for itself. Within the next few years the area should firm up well enough to determine its own course, to go on its own way—and we will then go ours.

These buildings were restored by private individuals who sought financial aid from Neighborhood Housing Services, Inc., in Pittsburgh.

These buildings dating from about 1870 offer potential in the Mexican War Streets area because they provide a variety of dwelling unit sizes ranging from two-story houses to efficiency apartments and contain a corner store. Pittsburgh History & Landmarks Foundation has acquired these buildings and plans to restore them for low- to moderate-income groups and to retain the beauty shop, operated by a black woman, and restore the interior.

1924 HARRIS & McKEEVER 1924
59 39 79
29 45 29
unify air conditioners behind overall louver
install new door and transom (existing out of scale)

A free restoration rendering prepared by the Pittsburgh Chapter, American Institute of Architects, showing an owner how to restore his Italianate commercial-residential building.

IX. A Concluding Note

This book leaves a great deal unanswered. I intend it only to suggest how you can begin your historic district program because information is not readily available on the subject.

I have not discussed many relevant matters such as historic zoning, specific programs in various cities, the use of easements (as carried out so well by Historic Annapolis) or the history of the preservation movement. My reason for so many omissions is simply that information is already available on those and other subjects. Again let me suggest that you write to the National Trust for Historic Preservation for their very fine list of available materials and bibliography of preservation literature. You will find appended to this volume a list of addresses of various agencies that can be of assistance to you.

This book is also meant to be a plea for a particular approach to historic preservation in cities. I am trying to suggest that preservationists widen their consciousness of the ingredients of such districts so that more attention can be paid to current residents, to the history of the district (in some historic districts that were historically integrated, for example, the preservationists segregated them into all white), to the street furniture, the vegetation, the street patterns and street life, all the things that make up a neighborhood, and then that restoration be carried out within that framework.

As preservationists we have no more right to "take over" a neighborhood than a redevelopment authority has; in earlier years the tools did not exist in the form of government programs to enable preservationists to retain low income residents in historic restoration districts, but they do now exist. It is our mission to see to it that architecturally significant structures are restored, protected, enlivened—that is all. But we must do so in the fairest and most useful way. How you might go about it is all that I want to indicate in these pages; there are and will be innumerable other ways, more expeditious, more effective, that can be utilized, and I urge you to try them out, always relating them to the givens of your neighborhood and the practicalities of your situation.

Addresses of some Agencies that can be useful to Historic Preservation Work.

Department of Housing and Urban Development
Washington, D. C. 20410

Federal Housing Administration
HUD Building
451 Seventh Street S. W.
Washington, D. C. 20410

Historic American Buildings Survey
National Park Service
801-10th Street
Washington, D.C.

Internal Revenue Service
1201 E Street N.W.
Washington, D. C. 20226

National Trust for Historic Preservation
748 Jackson Place N.W.
Washington, D. C. 20006

Society of Architectural Historians
1700 Walnut Street
Philadelphia, Pa. 19103

A great challenge: Victorian grandeur and solid housing, forlorn but intact in the ghetto area of Manchester in Pittsburgh.